WHEN KIDS GO WRONG

Help for Christian Parents

By

William J. Finnigan, D. Min.

"When Kids Go Wrong"
©William J. Finnigan, D. Min.
October 2023
Printed in the United States of America

ISBN: 979-8-9890422-2-7

Dr. Finnigan may be reached at:
8883 Sherwood Dr. NE
Warren, Ohio 44484
email: bilfinn1@yahoo.com

Formatting, Editing and Publishing Assisted By:
The Old Paths Publications, Inc.
Gainesville, Ga 30504
www.theoldpathspublications.com
email: TOP@theoldpathspublications.com

DEDICATION

3

To the vast company of Christian parents committed to raising their children in the fear, admonition, and joy of the LORD. (Ephesians 6:1-4)

TABLE OF CONTENTS

INTRODUCTION

"Except the LORD build the house, they labour in vain that build it…Lo, children are an heritage of the LORD: and the fruit of the womb is his reward." (Psalm 127:1,3)

These are momentous and challenging days to be alive! "Wars and rumors of war" characterize the condition of the world at large. Unrest and uncertainty are the order of the day; homes are shattered by divorce and rebellion, while churches suffer from spiritual lethargy and worldly intoxication. Parents and educators are struggling with an unprecedented growth of secularism and godlessness in our society. The breakdown of family structure and discipline has greatly contributed to the rise of delinquency, felonious assaults, and drug abuse, etc. The justice system has become increasingly corrupt as evidenced by our tolerance for criminal behavior and growing disdain for the police. The recent

"Covid-19 Pandemic" (so-called)` with all of its restrictions and mandates, etc. has only intensified the problems of family life.

A NEW LEVEL OF VIOLENCE

The country was shocked back at the turn of the century (1999) when two classmates at Columbine High School in Littleton, Colorado entered the building with guns and pipe bombs; they intended to wipe out the entire school population. When it was over, thirteen bodies were removed from the "war zone;" including the two murderers who later committed suicide. This frightful episode has made a profound and sobering mark on our society; so much so that books, documentaries, etc. have been produced to rehearse and analyze this horrific event. Certainly, as many thought, nothing like this would ever happen again; this was wishful thinking at best.

Some two decades later, tragedy struck again with even more intensity and devastation. Two young men, in separate incidents, massacred a number of innocent people; there were 10 shooting fatalities at a Buffalo, New York super market (5/14/22). Just ten days later, a second tragedy occurred (5/24/22) at an elementary school in Uvalde, Texas, leaving 19 children and 2 adults dead. What's going on in our society?

With the breakdown of our justice system and increasing disrespect for authority in general, I don't think we've "seen anything yet."

THE RESPONSIBILITY OF THE HOME

Since the home is the basic bastion for teaching obedience and respect, it's no wonder our country is imploding so quickly. We are gravely concerned about our "enemies" abroad (e.g. Russia, China, etc.) who threaten our national security; but in reality, the basic "enemy is us!"

Where are the fathers and mothers who take their "calling" and responsibility seriously? It doesn't take much to "father" a child, but being a father to a child is another matter. Parental failures, however, in no way exempt children who rebel and break the Law. But in these "last days', as God's judgment (Tribulation) approaches, believing dads and moms need to fully surrender to Jesus Christ; and begin "fighting" for the spiritual and emotional sanity of their families! This truth is especially vital in these troubled times when the power of Satan seems increasingly evident.

PAUL'S PROPHETIC WARNING

Hear Paul's prophetic message to young Timothy describing a new level of demonic wickedness in the *"last days."* (2 Timothy 3:1ff) *"Perilous times will come;"* i.e. days that are extremely troublesome, grievous, dangerous, savage (literally, hard to take). Consider this passage which reads like present day news:

> *For men shall be **lovers of their own selves**, covetous, boasters, proud, blasphemers, **disobedient***

> *to parents, **unthankful, unholy**, **Without natural affection**, trucebreakers, false accusers, incontinent, fierce, **despisers of those that are good**, Traitors, heady, highminded, **lovers of pleasures more than lovers of God**; **Having a form of godliness, but denying the power thereof:** from such turn away. (2 Timothy 3:2-5; emphasis mine)*

People have always been *"lovers of their own selves;"* and children have always been *"disobedient to parents, unthankful, unholy; without natural [common] affection, etc."* But we are witnessing an intensified, "snowballing" effect of these sins never seen before in our beloved land. It is heart-rending, alarming and downright scary! But it's a reality!

THE SEARCH FOR ANSWERS

There are some vital questions to be asked. Why are these tragedies happening? What is "ailing" our beloved country? Who's to blame? While I've mentioned Satan's desire to destroy us, we must not overlook the wicked people that he uses. We can't just blame the Devil per/se; but must take responsibility for playing into his hands by forsaking God and His Word. Unfortunately, we are reaping a harvest of wickedness stemming from our first sin sown in the Garden. (cf. Genesis 3)

Notice the acceleration of demonic rebellion among our young people. Violent crimes, assaults, and stealing, etc. have become common place. There's a "lawless" spirit dominating our society with a corresponding decline of law enforcement; in addition, there is an attitude of entitlement and victimization that has fostered laziness and personal irresponsibility. "You owe me" is the theme song; and if I don't get what I want, "it's your fault." "What's mine is mine; and what's yours is mine." This ungodly, selfish mentality has been fueled by our "progressive" government's ever-rising welfare "giveaways;" in turn this has served to "squelch" the God-given human work ethic of our present generation.

OBSESSION WITH VIOLENCE

In addition to the aforementioned problems, our country is demonically obsessed with violence of all sorts. Satan came to "kill, steal, and destroy" (John 10:10); this same mentality is becoming increasingly prevalent as our populace rejects God's Word. One factor to consider is the uninhibited use and addiction to violent video games. Society is constantly blaming "guns" for our crime waves; yet the same society thrives on movies that are filled with murder and violence. In our moral "sickness" we clamor for killing and vengeance, exacerbated by the various platforms of social media.

Another example of this demonic obsession is the increasing "frenzy" by some to confuse (and attempt to "change") sexual (gender) identity; such proponents only defy and scorn God's unique creation of *two* genders, i.e. male and female (Genesis 1:27); not to mention those who adamantly support the killing of babies in the womb!

This is a vast subject in itself; but it must be mentioned here because of its devastating influence on our children's education. Our present problem has much to do with the *indoctrination* (rather than education) of our children in left-winged, Bible-denying, and communistic learning institutions. In addition, just think of the power and influence of one iPhone in the hands of our children, potentially expos-ing them to the "whole" underworld! That's scary, indeed.

WHO CONTROLS OUR CHILDREN?

Must the children of God tolerate this satanic onslaught to destroy our God-given values of education? Do our children belong to us or to the State? This is a fundamental battle that must be faced squarely. In socialism, the government wants to "father" (i.e.

control) our children; thus, we all (including parents) become "ward" of the State; that's their socialistic goal! Our individual freedoms are subtly being "confiscated." So what do we do?

It must be observed that this present "dilemma" has been developing for many decades. The so-called "progressives" have been bucking our personal Constitutional freedoms in favor of socialistic government control. In other words, where we as individuals have failed to responsively practice and utilize our God-given liberty, it has been forfeited! When the populace refuses to take personal responsibility for its actions, "big brother" (government) is ready to pick up the slack.

The welfare system which intended to give the needy a "hand up" has now become a perpetual "hand out." Since the 1960s our beloved country has been rapidly "imploding" with all forms of corruption; including immorality, drug addiction, and domestic violence; not to mention sexual perversion, along with political, religious and educational deterioration.

ARE WE UNDER A CURSE?

Could it be, as some observe, that because of our utter rejection of God's Word (the Bible) we are under a satanic curse? Is our nation experiencing the judgment of God? When Israel forsook God's commandments they became subject to the gods of destruction, sexual perversion and child sacrifice (e.g. Exodus 32; Numbers 25:1-18; Judges 10:6-16). Could it be that the Enemy has taken the above scenario (idolatry) to a new level of intensity and deception today? Modern invention and technology has certainly made the "gods" of this world more accessible; but that is also true of the "light of the Gospel." The choice between "light" and "darkness" stares us in the face!

Jesus speaks of a demon spirit gone out of a man and walking over dry land, seeking rest; finding none, he decides to return to the his "house" (human body) from which he came; finding it "empty," he invites seven other demons, "more wicked then himself" to dwell with him; and Jesus says, "the last state of that man is worse than the first. Even so shall it be also unto this wicked generation." (cf. Matthew 12:43-45)

Does this not give a "snapshot" analysis of what's happening to our beloved country? America in the past has been a bulwark and disperser of Biblical truth; this has resulted in the restraining and "chasing out" the gods of corruption and open wickedness. But obviously, that is not the case at present. In fact, as the above-mentioned man, "delivered" of demons and then "repossessed;" so is the fate of our once-great nation; only now the "latter end" is worse than the beginning! It is in this "atmosphere," by the grace of God, that Christian families today must thrive.

HEAR THE SCRIPTURE!

Gratefully, the Apostle Paul gives us some insight in the above-mentioned prophetic passage regarding the "last days" in 2 Timothy 3. In the midst of turbulent circumstances, Paul exhorts young Timothy to continue to focus and rest in *"the holy Scriptures which are able to make thee wise unto salvation…"* (2 Timothy 3:15) Then he reminds him (us) of God's bed-rock, super-natural, all-sufficient gift of the Word of God:

> *All scripture is given by inspiration of God, and is profitable for doctrine, for reproof, for correction, for instruction in righteousness: That the man of God may be perfect, throughly furnished unto all good works. (2 Timothy 3:16 & 17)*

The Lord has provided His Word (the Bible) to sustain and feed His children in the worst of situations. This is borne out throughout church history; and is presently being demonstrated by persecuted believers suffering in various parts of the world. In this light, the need for godly, Bible-based homes is paramount. Consider that Satan's first attack on Job was to destroy his family. Things haven't changed!

We must not back down nor forsake God's beautiful institution of marriage; i.e. the joining of a man and a woman in a God-covenant relationship to establish a home and family. This is basic to the well-being of our society. A solid Christian home is our "fortress" against the onslaughts of Hell.

(*Check our website for a helpful resource on "The Family;" a free ebook, https://www.billfinnigan.com)

ARE CHILDREN ALWAYS "VICTIMS"?

The focus on building strong Christian homes, however, does not automatically insure a "successful" family life. Considering that every member of the family is imperfect, home-life can easily become a spiritual battleground. The best of Christian parents fall short, along with the children:

*For all have sinned, and come short
of the glory of God; (Romans 3:23)*

Believing parents have the God-given ministry of leading their children by example and instruction. We pray earnestly that in time each child comes to a saving knowledge of Jesus Christ; but in the interim that home may experience many episodes of spiritual, emotional, and physical conflict.

HANDLING REBELLION

What happens, for instance, when a child begins to stray and balk at parental authority, etc.? Modern psychology is quick to blame the parents for a child's waywardness; or falsely relegate "rebellion" as a "mental disorder." (more on this later) Needless to say, every parent has failed in the awesome task of child-rearing; the problem with children is much deeper than parental guidance. Could the term "dysfunctional" actually apply to every family, to one degree or another? Just asking?

It's essential to understand that every child possesses the Adamic sin nature which is the source of his/her ungodly behavior.

> *Wherefore, as by one man sin entered into the world, and death by sin; and so death passed upon all men, for that all have sinned. (cf. Romans 5:12)*

Yes, I know it's heart-wrenching to believe that those "darling, sweet" little ones are rebels against God's authority. It doesn't take long for any honest parent to witness their child's true, fallen nature. Remember, while your children are born with your DNA, that does *not* include your regenerated "spirit;" that comes only through the Holy Spirit's "new birth" in salvation. God has no "grandchildren." No one gets to Heaven on his/her mother's "apron string."

Therefore, we must conclude that children are not always "victims;" when they do wrong, they need to be held responsible for their sinful behavior;

discipline must be swiftly, wisely and fairly administered. (cf. Ephesians 6:1-4; Proverbs 13:24) As we will see, godly parents are quick to take blame for a child's misconduct; but to make parents a "scapegoat" is wrong. We need to face this issue squarely, considering the role and responsibility of all members of the family.

The fight is on! Satan's attack on the home is relentless. There is no way that parents can monitor their children 24/7. As mentioned above, despite the imperfections of parents, children must take responsibility for their attitude and actions. Every child has a conscience, thus knowing right from wrong. As we'll see, being godly responsible parents does not guarantee the salvation of their children. All "kids" are born in sin and need a Savior; that will not happen apart from the regenerating work of the Holy Spirit. Likewise, children raised in "ungodly" homes are still responsible for their sinful behavior. In either case, these "kids" should never be labeled as victims.

WHAT ABOUT MENTAL DISORDERS?

One catastrophic "reality" in our present society is to confuse sin with "mental illness." We are excusing lawless and anti-social behavior under the guise of psychological "disorders." While all people have some level of "mental difficulty," that never justifies immoral conduct. If our kids have so-called "mental disorders" like "hyperactivity" or Autism, etc., the tendency is to minimize the reality and/or consequence of the child's misbehavior. That's a subtle mistake.

Now, instead of leading them to the Cross for forgiveness, etc. we simply give them some psychotropic (brain-altering) medication. This is not to say that there are no legitimate uses for psychological "meds;" but to mask a child's sinful behavior by "medication" is not only wrong, but criminal! Remember that Jesus didn't die for "Schizophrenia" per/se, but for *Sin*! No "medicinal" remedy can ever "substitute" for Christ's saving work at the Cross!

The truth is that society at large, including the mental health community, has no satisfactory explanation as to "why kids go wrong." As we've seen, a teen-age boy procures a rifle, and decides to "shoot up" an elementary school; strict gun laws are no deterrent to anyone determined to get a gun. This "kid" comes from a stable family; he has no record of "mental issues," etc. He becomes a "mass murderer," to the consternation and embarrassment of his family and all other associations. How do you explain this tragedy?

A HEART ISSUE

There's no psychiatric textbook or mental health "expert" that can fathom or remedy the above phenomenon. A child is born not only with his parents' DNA, but also their sin nature. The Bible says,

The heart [nature] is deceitful above all things and desperately wicked; who can know it. (Jeremiah 17:9)

We all do what we do because we are what we are! Children may conform to external guidelines at home, school, etc., but the power of sin and Satan still lurks in the mind. Jesus' pungent description of the human heart (nature) is foundational to understanding the basis of human corruption. He says that:

*There is nothing from without a man, that entering into him can defile him: but the things which **come out of him**, **those** are they that **defile the man**... For **from within, out of the heart** of men, **proceed evil** thoughts, adulteries, fornications, **murders**, **thefts**, covetousness, **wickedness,** deceit, lasciviousness, an evil eye, blasphemy, pride, foolishness: **All these evil things come from within, and defile the man.** (cf. Mark 7:15, 21-23; emphasis mine)*

It's not a pretty picture, is it? But that's the reality of the human heart without Christ. The world of humanism will not accept this truth; rather it dodges the issue, seeking ever to "excuse" and/or "reform" sinful behavior. According to Jesus' words, a person is not a thief because he steals; but he steals because he's a thief. One is not a murderer because he kills; but he kills because he's a murderer! The first baby born, Cain, grew up only to murder his brother Abel in an angry rebellious fit! (cf. Genesis 4:3f) This was a "preview of coming attractions" in the history of mankind.

We'd like to think that our "sweet bundle of joy" is born in a "neutral" state, just awaiting our parental development skills, etc. Surprise! We soon observe, as King David testified,

> *Behold, I was shapen in iniquity;*
> *and in sin did my mother conceive*
> *me. (Psalm 51:5)*

No honest parent has ever taught his child to do wrong; they do that automatically. Sin is "built in" and thus expressed "naturally."

THE PARENTAL CHALLENGE

The ongoing challenge for godly parents is to prayerfully point their children to Christ, while anticipating God's "supernatural" intervention. We face a monumental task as parents (and adults) to rightly teach and influence our young people. Our daily testimony speaks volumes to those who follow us; indeed, we are building bridges for the next generation. The increasing rise of divorce and single-parenting has paid a toll. Homes with the stability of a father and mother are waning all too rapidly. Too many children are "fending for themselves," becoming inundated with the ungodly forces available on television, videos, and social media.

Remember, our kids have a fallen nature that, apart from God's restraining grace, gravitates to the satanic "underworld;" And amazingly all this "material" is available on one iPhone! Unfortunately, too often biblical discipline and moral absolutes have been replaced by permissiveness and "self-esteem" development. Modern psychology is not producing the goods! It behooves even responsible parents to stop being "buddies" to their children; and become godly role models who manage the home with loving authority.

Loving justice begins at home. The courts are in trouble because the home is in trouble. When I was a boy, dads basically ruled the household. Curfews were set and children all had responsibilities with household chores and schoolwork. Neighbors cooperated with each other's children. For instance, if a neighbor boy was seen smoking, he was reprimanded and his father notified. There was a system of checks and balances in the community. The police were not involved in domestic disputes except in extreme cases. Fathers, by and large, controlled the household, making it easier on teachers and law enforcement officers.

We have lost respect for authority without which our society cannot be maintained. While the economy seems to flourish, war rages in human hearts. As already stated, the judgment of God is upon our nation because we have forsaken the God of our fathers!

> *Righteousness exalteth a nation, but sin is a reproach to any people (Proverbs 14:36).*

It's time to get back to biblical basics, not only at school but at home.

DISILLUSIONED PARENTS

But what about parents who have brought up children in the "nurture and admonition of the Lord" only to be disappointed and disillusioned at the results? Isn't God true to His Word? Is there anyone else besides me who thought that if a parent followed certain biblical precepts the children would automatically come through for God? After all, doesn't Proverbs 22:6 make it clear that if I *"train up a child in the way he should go"* that even when he's old "he will not depart from it?"

This whole issue needs to be addressed in light of the multitudes of defeated and guilt-laden parents whose hearts bleed for their wayward children ("kids"). Most suffer silently; and for too long we have been silent about the problem. Few Christian parents suffering under depression, etc. are eager to share their burden with others; they are embarrassed and fearful of being labeled as "failures."

So many godly parents suffer quietly in public, living in defeat because they can't figure out what went wrong. Guilt overwhelms their hearts and opens the door for satanic accusation and oppression. They can't even testify to the goodness of the Lord because they now question whether He really is "good" and answers prayer.

This is especially true when folks stand up in church and testify how they dedicated their children to the Lord as infants; and that's why they grew up to serve God. What trauma and pain such a testimony inflicts upon a faithful parent who likewise dedicated his/her child to the Lord only to see him run from God! Immediately there's the guilt syndrome like, "where did I mess up?" It's like the person who testifies of God's healing while another has sought the same God and yet remains sick. What's going on? Why doesn't it work the same for everybody? These questions can bring disillusionment if we're not anchored to the Rock of Ages.

Let's be clear, children are an inheritance from the Lord (Psalm 127); therefore, parents have an awesome responsibility and privilege to demonstrate the grace of God before them. There is no way to minimize the necessity for godly training and influence. However, we must understand that children are sinners from birth;

> *The wicked are estranged from the womb: they go astray as soon as they be born, speaking lies (Psalm 58:3);*

That is, they are individual moral agents, knowing right from wrong. We must conclude here that the process of child- rearing is not as simplistic and neatly packaged as some "experts" would make it.

NO SIMPLE ANSWER

I suspect that things would be far different if we as parents could be the "Holy Spirit" to our children. I thought as a young father that if I instructed my family daily in the Word, lived Christ before them, went to the ball games and school activities, wrestled with them on the floor, etc. etc., that they would all someday line up to serve God. I must tell you that it hasn't quite worked that way for me; understand, however, that I'm ever grateful for the abundant evidence of God's saving grace He has bestowed thus far; and, yes, the "story isn't over yet."

Now I know a few families who seem to evidence a whole "household salvation;" this is so encouraging to witness, and I gladly rejoice with them in celebrating God's goodness. However, that does not relieve the burden for other families where parents have likewise tried to be a godly example. Some might retort, "But you must have missed it somewhere along the way as a parent;" to which I and others would reply, "you're right, but so did those other folks." I'm sure that those parents with an outstanding family situation would be quick to give God the glory for what He's done in their home; not because of all they did right, but in spite of all the ways they "missed it!".

Even Jesus pleaded with his people when he cried in Matthew 23:37:

O, Jerusalem, Jerusalem,...how often would I have gathered thy children together, even as a hen gathereth her chickens under her wings, and ye would not!

They were not willing to come to him though he was the embodiment of love and compassion. How this epitomizes a parent's heart-cry for a wayward child! Let's face it, good parenting does not guarantee good children.

DILEMMA OF CHILD-REARING

The Scriptures are replete with examples of godly fathers who had wicked sons. (e.g. Isaac, Aaron, Eli, Samuel, David, etc.) On the other hand, there are examples of wicked fathers who had godly off-spring.(e.g. Joash, Hezekiah, Josiah, etc.) I know of families riddled by divorce, drugs, etc. and yet the children are serving God today. That doesn't seem right, but it's a fact; and praise God for it! Certainly our God is in he business of "bringing fruit out of a garbage pail;" it's called *Grace*!

Parents are often exhorted to: "Hang in there, the story's not over yet." I agree that such a statement fosters great consolation and hope; but it must not become just a "spiritual cliché." We must still consider the prospect of having children that may choose to reject Christ. But you say: "Claim them for Jesus and never give up for household salvation is promised in Acts 16:31."

> *And they said, Believe on the Lord Jesus Christ, and thou shalt be saved, and thy house.*

Yes, many true believers "cling" to this verse, and yet they live in the dilemma of "unanswered" prayer!

"ANSWERED PRAYER" SYNDROME

We hear people testify how "God always answers all their prayers…" That's always fascinated me, seeing that I've struggled in the prayer chamber for over 50 years and still have not seen certain prayers answered. Don't misunderstand, God *does* answer prayer; and praise be to Him for His gracious undertaking in my life! But one who testifies that "all his prayers are answered" falls into one of the following categories: a) he/she is a "super-saint" on a lofty spiritual plane; b) one who is deceived about the answers; c) a flat-out liar; or d) one who doesn't pray much!

The "answered prayer" syndrome is no simple matter to handle. We are all faced with the reality of the omnipotent and Holy God who has an infinite plan and timing for our lives. Much teaching today suggests that all we must do is "ring the bell and God comes running" to our aid. The truth is that it's God that "rings the bell and *we* come running!" No amount of prayer can "twist" the arm of a Sovereign God. We must walk in humble obedience to Him and thus pray according to His will (I John 5:14f).

PROPER UNDERSTANDING OF SCRIPTURE

Care must be taken to rightly divide God's word in every area, without forcing unwarranted meanings into the text. A typical example is Proverbs 22:6, which states:

> *Train up a child in the way he should go and when he is old he will not depart from it.*

Along with many, I have used this verse as a "guarantee" to insure my family's salvation before God. Looking back, however, I've wondered if I had rightly interpreted that proverb? Is it a "promise" of eternal salvation resulting from "training up a child" to learn how to live? The context rather states a "principle" (axiom) of effective child-rearing in light of future maturity and development. Certainly, any Christian parent would gladly *apply* this "training" process to include pointing their child to the Savior.

Keep in mind that Proverbs, like Psalms, is a poetical book. It magnifies the character of God and sets forth principles that govern the human race on earth. For example, Proverbs 15:1 says,

A soft answer turneth away wrath:
but grievous words stir up anger.

At first glance one might interpret that verse to mean that answering an angry man with "soft" (gentle) words will definitely deter his anger. That may happen, but don't depend on it! This is *not* a promise, but a general axiom or principle; it's teaching us "not to fight fire with fire;" it's an attempt to "disarm" an angry person with a gentle, kind response; hopefully to "overcome evil with good."

OUR HOPEFUL STRUGGLE

Let's consider Solomon's classic exhortation to:

Train up a child in the way he
should go: and when he is old, he

*will not depart from it. Proverbs
22:6*

The word "train" is a verb meaning first "to put something into the mouth;" "to give to be tasted," as pre- masticated food given by a nurse to an infant. It then took on the meaning of "giving elementary instruction" or "to train."

The Hebrew is literally: "Initiate a child in accordance with his way. ...'*His way*' must mean one of two things—either his future calling and station, or his character, natural inclination and capacity." (Pulpit Commentary, Vol. 9) The latter description seems to fit the context, but not without the basic training in obedience and morality. Thus, the Hebrew text adds "**even** *when he is old, he will not depart from it.*"

This training will bear fruit all of his life, becoming second nature; however, let it be known that "salvation is of the Lord," and the parent can never play the role of the Holy Spirit. Each child must still make a conscious choice before God regarding his soul's destiny.

This understanding in no way can ever nullify or justify any parental failure to "bring up our children in the nurture and admonition of the Lord" (see Ephesians 6:4). Rather it should encourage every parent to fervently and faithfully intercede in prayer for their children. Parents **and** children are **both** responsible to obey and submit to God Almighty.

SOLOMON'S DISAPPOINTMENT

Is it not significant that Solomon himself strayed from his father David's instruction and met with God's severe discipline (2 Kings 11)? In Proverbs, Solomon directly uses the term "my son" twenty-three times in exhorting his boy. For instance, in Proverbs 23:26, he says,

My son, give me thine heart, and let thine eyes observe my ways.

Unfortunately, when his son Rehoboam took the throne, he rejected his father's instruction; and brought great shame to Solomon and the God of his fathers (I Kings 12).

What a grievous situation. Solomon knew God's abundant provision firsthand and wanted so much to share that with his son. Thus, he wanted his son's heart so he could relinquish everything else. How we lose out when we refuse to submit to a father's love and counsel!

I am not suggesting for a moment that God doesn't honor and use a parent's effort to nurture his children spiritually. Every attempt must be made in this regard, but the eternal results can only be left in God's hands. How many parents see their children in church with a seeming godly testimony and outward moral behavior; only to find out later that they were hypocrites (i.e. actors)! Things are not always what they appear to be. We must trust God fully, even when the "ducks don't line up" the way we think they should.

FACING THE TRUTH

I know parents who testify: "All my children are saved; they've all made professions of faith, but are not living for the Lord." Likewise, we hear of those who were "saved and baptized when they were 12 years old but are just backsliders." Is this really a genuine Biblical concept when true salvation is evidenced by a "new creation" and godly desire? (2 Corinthians 5:17) Is "profession" of faith the same as the "possession" of faith? How long can one be a "backslider" without manifesting some genuine evidence of true salvation? (e.g. Galatians 5:22&23) I wonder how many so-called "backsliders" have ever really "slid-forward?"

Frankly, over the years I've witnessed the true conversion of so-called "backsliders" who were hiding behind an empty "decision" or false "profession" of faith; but later were convinced by the Holy Spirit that they had never experienced the "new birth."

This is a serious issue! It might be shocking to know how many "professing" Christians in our churches have never been truly converted to Christ.

When it comes to our children, it's difficult for a parent to be totally honest regarding a child's true spiritual condition. This is a touchy subject in that we have a tendency to project our pride in and through our children. We all want our "kids" to do well in every way; for this reason, it's difficult to tell "the whole truth" when asked about their well-being; it's often convenient just to answer, "They're doing fine, thanks," avoiding the details.

Years ago, I remember speaking to a young man about the Lord after a church service. He readily acknowledged his sin and need for salvation. His mother, who overheard the conversation, abruptly stepped up between us and angrily said to me, "My boy is a good boy and not a sinner." With that she grabbed him by the arm and whisked him away.

How sad! Let's face it, that mother's pride was offended, to think that anyone would "accuse" her son of being anything other than a "good boy."

How tough it is to admit that our children are not where they should be spiritually. As parents we feel responsible for our children in every aspect. They are reflections of us and if not living for God, they foster suspicion in others as to the success of our parenting; not to mention the onslaught of condemning accusations from Satan.

Some Christian parents are satisfied if their children grow up to be upright, responsible adults; while other parents are expecting their children to demonstrate a vibrant testimony for Christ in whatever their field of endeavor. No, they need not become "full-time" Christian workers per/se; but in whatever vocation they choose a genuine love for Christ should be evident.

THREE OPTIONS

It seems to me that there are three basic approaches to this parental dilemma. The *first* option is to live under a constant "guilt trip," putting ourselves down and succumbing to defeat. This is the typical response of sincere, honest and serious parents. It not only robs their joy and effectiveness in ministry but opens the door for depression and demonic attack. These are the people who attempt to serve the Lord in embarrassing defeat because their children have disgraced them and their God. They feel totally disqualified to testify of God's goodness because of their devastated home situation.

The *second* option is to live in denial and apply the so-called "carnal Christian" theory. This position supposes that salvation is equated with a "decision for Christ" or "profession of faith" without any connection with resultant behavior. In other words, even though there's no change of life or desire to follow God, this person is "saved and on his way to Heaven." We've all known people (young and old) who have professed Christ but manifest no lifestyle change or desire for God; this flies in the face of Scripture which insists that

> *if any man be in Christ, he is a new creature; old things are passed away; behold, all things are become new (2 Corinthians 5:17)!*

Thus the parent taking this approach would say: "My boy asked Jesus into his heart when he was nine and I know he's saved." In other words, the boy really has no semblance of true life in God and is even rebellious; yet he must be "saved" because of his "profession of faith." At best, we might say that he's "backslidden;" but could it be possible, as mentioned above, that our teenage "backslider" never really "slid" forward? I know it's painful to consider that possibility; but remember that God doesn't produce "still-births;" There must be some evidence of spiritual life in conversion. Certainly it's easier to live in denial, assuming that all is well; but that can only lead to deception and disaster.

It might be best to take the **third** option and face the situation squarely for what it is. What a difficult "pill" to swallow, to think that my children could be anything but "saved." Yet, we must acknowledge the present reality of our family and take whatever "lumps" necessary. But let's do so without living in guilt, accusation, defeat or denial. Let's consider the fact that there's still victory in Jesus regardless of our circumstance. We must go on regardless of the warfare. I agree that the story is not over yet!

THE CAIN AND ABEL SYNDROME

Since society increasingly rejects the sin nature principle in people generally, and in children particularly, any fault-finding can only be leveled at parents. The psychologists are masters in blaming environment, genetic predisposal and dysfunctional families for all our woes. Without an understanding of a child's basic nature there's no adequate explanation as to why kids do what they do. Psychological theories will not suffice in addressing the plague of youthful offenders and rebels in our day. "Sin" has become a nasty word and yet it remains at the very heart of the problem. We need to get back to basics and rediscover what God says about the issue. We've already established the truth that every child comes into this world as a liar, a rebel and a deceiver! (cf. Psalm 51:5; 58:3; Jeremiah 17:9; Romans 3:10-12).

> ***Psalm 51:5*** *Behold, I was shapen in iniquity; and in sin did my mother conceive me.*

> ***Psalm 58:3*** *The wicked are estranged from the womb: they go astray as soon as they be born, speaking lies.*

> ***Jeremiah 17:9*** *The heart is deceitful above all things, and*

desperately wicked: who can know it?

Romans 3:10 *As it is written, There is none righteous, no, not one:* **11** *There is none that understandeth, there is none that seeketh after God.* **12** *They are all gone out of the way, they are together become unprofitable; there is none that doeth good, no, not one.*

But you say: "If our children just had the right environment and proper education, they would make it." Wait a minute! Where does a child have any more opportunity for the above than right here in America? It doesn't get any better than this, and yet look at the mess we're in. We've conducted blitz campaigns to "educate" them on the perils of smoking, illicit sex and drugs; but to no avail.

The problem is that education fails to change a wicked and rebellious heart, bent on destruction. Our prisons are filled with brilliant, educated people who "know" better, but refuse to do right!

This could even be said of the average student in our Christian schools, who is taught the Word of God, right from wrong, etc. but chooses to walk in the opposite direction.

Just recently, a heroin addict told me that he was brought up under the Word of God at home and at church; however, he said when his parents instructed him "to go right, he went left!" O, how deep, how far reaching and tragic is the nature of sin!

Should we be shocked at the present state of affairs? Yes, but only if we are ignorant of God's historical commentary on man's beginning. Adam and Eve were created to live in a perfect environment called the Garden of Eden (Genesis 3). They walked in delightful fellowship with their Creator until one day they rebelled against God, deciding to live independently from Him. How could one ever sin in a "perfect" environment; but it happened! They were instructed (or educated) to do right and placed in a beautiful garden; yet despite every advantage they chose to disobey. That's where sin on earth began.(cf. Romans 5:12)

> **Romans 5:12** *Wherefore, as by one man sin entered into the world, and death by sin; and so death passed upon all men, for that all have sinned:*

Presumably, the first couple repented after being exposed by the Lord; by grace He provided them a skin-covering from an animal sacrifice to cover their sinful nakedness (Genesis 3:21). It wasn't long before the first two boys arrived on the planet, i.e. Cain and Abel. Significantly, both boys had the same parents and were equally instructed about God's way of salvation. Yet, Abel obeyed, and Cain didn't.

They were both brought up in a near-perfect environment; yet rebellion was still evident in Cain's heart. He had the same opportunity to believe (obey) God as did Abel, but he refused. Whose fault was it? Was it dad's problem, thus making Adam responsible for Cain's response? Was it the environment? Was it Abel's "better choice" that forced Cain to be envious? Or maybe it was God's problem in that He (God) was too demanding; thus, victimizing the young lad.

The truth is that Cain was a godless, arrogant rebel who would not believe God! Why are we so surprised when kids go wrong? They're wrong to begin with because of sin. When will we squarely accept this fact? Children are depraved sinners like anyone else. Only the grace of God through the Gospel of Jesus Christ can save those who repent and believe. The change must come from **within** rather than the mere outward conformity to rules. *Religion* can be likened to a dead man's attempt to reach ***up*** for the living God, but he cannot reach that high. *Salvation*, however, is the living God reaching **down** for a dead man, and He can reach that low! (cf. John 3:16)

GOD'S GRIEF OVER HIS DISOBEDIENT CHILDREN

Believe it or not, even God has disobedient children. The entire Old Testament is replete with examples of God's loving and grief-stricken heart; He was forever calling wayward Israel to repent and return to Him. One of the most vivid pictures of this is found in Isaiah's writing:

> *Hear, O heavens, and give ear, O earth: for the LORD hath spoken, I have nourished and brought up children, and they have rebelled against me. The ox knoweth his owner, and the ass his master's crib: but Israel doth not know, my people doth not consider.   Ah sinful nation, a people laden with in-iniquity, a seed of evildoers, children that are corrupters: they have forsaken the LORD, they have provoked the Holy One of Israel unto anger, they are gone away backward. (Isaiah 1:2-4)*

The Lord calls heaven and earth to witness the tragic condition of His children. The whole creation beckons to His commands, but not humanity! Those whom He called and nurtured have rebelled against their Father. Yet the ox and donkey know their master; they appreciate and serve their owner. It's incredible that a farmer should get more love and obedience from an animal than God Almighty gets from His children!

Likewise, children have no idea how a father's heart is delighted when a son (child) obeys. (cf. Proverbs 10:1) What release of love and joy is made possible when a father and son are on track together. Solomon prayed for wisdom to lead the people; but in addition, God "threw in" riches and blessing beyond measure. He's the same One who said:

> *Seek ye first the kingdom of God...and all these things shall be added unto you (Matthew 6:33).*

Oh, if we only knew by experience the riches of His grace and what we're missing when we fail to obey!

The agnostic might say that if God has disobedient children, then something must be radically wrong with His training procedures. He must have been lacking in parenting skills, etc. What a ridiculous accusation to level at the Most High God! Instead, check the depth of rebellion and corruption of His so-called "children." To think that the omnipotent God who rules the universe would even tolerate for a moment such rebellion to His love, is beyond comprehension!

Significantly, we witness God's empathy with Jewish parents with obstinate children; under Mosaic Law, it was a capital offense for a son to be "stubborn and rebellious" to parental authority. An incorrigible son could be taken by his parents to the elders for "capital punishment" by stoning. (cf. Deuteronomy 21: 18-21) Undoubtedly, such action would reinforce parental authority and reestablish the "fear of God" in children. Apart from the "execution" aspect, we need some application of this law today.

SIN'S DECEPTION

Isaiah likens these people to the "sodomites" of old who were notorious for their pride and perversion (Isaiah 1:10). He further challenges the validity of their religious rituals saying: "To what purpose is the multitude of your sacrifices unto me, saith the Lord: I am full of [literally, fed up with] the burnt offerings...." (vs.11) Here they were going through the religious motions just as if nothing was wrong. They attempted to keep up the righteous facade, when all the while their hearts were full of "Hell."

Why didn't God just give up on these folks? Good question, but the fact is He didn't. Rather, with a father's heart of grief, He pleads with them again:

> *Come now, and let us reason together, saith the LORD: though your sins be as scarlet, they shall be as white as snow; though they be red like crimson, they shall be as*

wool. If ye be willing and obedient, ye shall eat the good of the land: But if ye refuse and rebel, ye shall be devoured with the sword: for the mouth of the LORD hath spoken it. (Isaiah 1:18-20)

The term *"let us reason together"* does not mean simply "talking it over with God;" rather it entails acknowledging and then dealing with the issue at hand. Sin is deceptive, causing one to live a lie with no conviction of iniquity; there must come a spiritual awakening if one is to "come" to the Lord. Graciously God offers them cleansing and forgiveness if they repent. To refuse is to jeopardize their eternal souls.

A SOLEMN APPEAL

Providentially, the present reader may be one who is not only estranged from God, but from family. Please consider the above admonition seriously. God invites those who are "willing" to "come" and receive his forgiving grace;

yes, to make your "scarlet sin" as "white as snow;" and then placing you into His heavenly Kingdom. How wonderful is that?

Acknowledge your rebellion and receive the Lord Jesus Christ by faith while there's yet time! (cf. John 1:12; Romans 10:9&10)

> ***John 1:12*** *But as many as received him, to them gave he power to become the sons of God, even to them that believe on his name:*

> ***Romans 10:9*** *That if thou shalt confess with thy mouth the Lord Jesus, and shalt believe in thine heart that God hath raised him from the dead, thou shalt be saved.* ***10*** *For with the heart man believeth unto righteousness; and with the mouth confession is made unto salvation.*

Then, like the "prodigal son" (or daughter), you can go "home" and be reconciled with family.

This is a most solemn matter. Do not trifle with your eternal soul which is precious in God's sight! Don't continue to spurn the love of God and the heart-cry of parents and friends who have prayed for you. "Behold, now is the accepted time; behold, *now* is the day of salvation!" (2 Corinthians 6:2)

Years ago, as a young father, I heard a true story that moved my heart. A widow had three grown sons, which she and her late husband raised in the ways of God. She gathered them one day to share her heart, saying:

"Boys, I have tried my best over the years to raise you in the fear and admonition of the Lord. I love each of you dearly and have attempted to be the best mother possible. I have shared my heart with you along with God's precious Word. It's up to you now to decide whom you will serve: yourself or God. If you choose your own way, you do so at the jeopardy of your eternal soul."

She went on to explain that her prayers and continued love for them would remain as long as she had breath.

But one day, she said, we'll all stand before God and give an account of our lives. If at that time you are still unrepentant (unsaved), the day of Grace will be expired; and you will face God's eternal judgment in Hell.

As parents, we can only recoil at such a dreadful thought! O that it would never come to that! But let it be known that this mother's burden is valid and shared by many; our children are no less accountable to the Lord than anyone else's children. He (the Lord) is "no respecter of persons;" Christ is not only the loving Saviour to those who repent and believe, but a *"consuming fire"* to those who reject Him! (cf. Hebrews 12:29) Remember Paul's words,

> *Be not deceived; God is not mocked; for whatsoever a man soweth that shall he also reap..* (Galatians 6:7)

In reality, it's time for parents and children alike to urgently consider the prophet's exhortation:

Seek ye the LORD while He may be found; call ye upon Him while He is near. Let the wicked forsake his way, and the unrighteous man his thoughts: and let him return unto the LORD, and he will have mercy upon him…and He will abundantly pardon. (Isaiah 55:6&7)

Dear reader, whatever your station in life, please listen; consider that God took your lost condition seriously when He sent His Son Jesus Christ to suffer your judgment upon the Cross. Now it's your turn to take Him seriously while there's yet time; if you've never experienced His saving grace, cry out to Him now in repentant faith.

Hear Fanny Crosby's penitent hymn:

PASS ME NOT

*Pass me not, O gentle Savior, hear my humble cry;
*While on others Thou art calling, do not pass me by.
*Let me at a throne of mercy, find a sweet relief;

*Kneeling there in deep contrition, help my unbelief.
*Trusting only in Thy merit, would I seek Thy face;
*Heal my wounded, broken spirit, save me by Thy grace.

PRACTICAL SUGGESTIONS FOR PARENTS

In conclusion, let us consider some practical insights in facing the ongoing challenge of raising our children:

1) *Never give up*!
There's a God in Glory who still hears the cry of His saints. While the children have breath there is still hope. They cannot "outrun" the Holy Spirit! Pray that God would send another believer to share the Word with that child; thus re- confirming what you have taught.

Some years ago, a friend wrote of his personal encounter with the son of the great prayer-warrior E.M. Bounds. Prompted by the Spirit, he made an appointment to visit with Osborne Bounds who was then in his eighties. On that occasion my friend pressed home the Gospel to this preacher's son and there he opened his heart to Christ. That was 63 years after his father's death! It's too soon to give up on your children.

2) *Intercede for each child daily at the throne of Grace.*

We are in constant "battle" for their souls against the Destroyer himself (John 10:10)! Name their names, one by one, and ask God to put His thoughts into their minds. Stand in resistant faith against the adversary. Fight the good fight of faith!

3) *Get rid of all resentment in your heart.*

Face your situation squarely. Warfare always produces casualties and a primary one here is bitterness toward God and/or your children. Please don't ignore or reject this possibility. You will do so at the cost of your own sanity and spiritual victory. You have labored in prayer, searched your heart, etc., but nothing seems to change. Remember, we don't really know what God is doing "behind the scenes."

Keep a sweet spirit, refusing to develop any issues or bitterness toward God. Cleverly, Satan would plant slanderous thoughts in your mind regarding "God's goodness, etc." Such unbelieving accusations regarding God's faithfulness will greatly hamper your fellowship with the only One who can change the circumstance. Don't let that happen!

In turn, any resentment toward your children will sour your relationship together and impede progress. Thus, confess to God your resentment toward Him and your children (I John 1:9). As God leads, make restitution with each child, confessing your sinful and resentful attitude. Reassure them of your unconditional love for them personally, though you may not approve of their lifestyle.

4) *Maintain a victorious attitude in Christ.*

Quit punishing yourself! If there's genuine guilt about something, deal with it before God and move on. It is imperative to enjoy the Lord in ongoing fellowship regardless of the circumstance. We don't have to be "bent out of shape" just because our "ducks don't line up." In fact, our misery can only serve to make matters worse; among other things, it will sap our spiritual stamina and ability to pray effectively. Let us be Spirit-filled testimonies of Christ while He conducts His ministry in our family!

5) *Enjoy and appreciate your children regardless of their spiritual condition.*

They are God's gift to you and therefore are unique people. Love them, for they are not "mistakes." Do not wall yourself off, but rather encourage and wisely help them as you can. Let them clearly witness the unique power of Christ in your life.

6) *Take the "praise" challenge which is faith in action!*

Give God the glory because you're a survivor, i.e. you've come through the storm of suffering. You are growing in grace and learning to "rejoice in tribulation" which produces "patience, experience and hope" (Romans 5:2-4).

You are in the process of experiencing the faithfulness of our Heavenly Father who exemplifies what a parent should be. Suffering has a purpose and "we are more than conquerors" in the midst of the battle! You have a *message* that others need to hear. Don't faint! (Luke 18:1)

> **Luke 18:1** *And he spake a parable unto them to this end, that men ought always to pray, and not to faint;*

7)   *Be thankful to God for children who manifest true godliness.*
This applies to your "kids" or someone else's. Encourage them in their walk with God that they might shine brightly in their daily environment. Likewise, bless

and encourage parents who are going through deep water with their kids. You can minister grace to them because of God's grace and comfort given to you. (cf. 2 Corinthians 1:3,4)

> ***2 Corinthians 1:3*** *Blessed be God, even the Father of our Lord Jesus Christ, the Father of mercies, and the God of all comfort;* ***4*** *Who comforteth us in all our tribulation, that we may be able to comfort them which are in any trouble, by the comfort wherewith we ourselves are comforted of God.*

8)   *Be on the lookout for children who are open for truth.*

Your young person may be closed-minded right now, but you could be the "answer to prayer" for another parent. God may just place someone's child in your path at the right time to influence them for Christ.

Some years ago, as a college professor, I witnessed the miraculous conversion of one of my students. Unbeknown to me, the Holy Spirit was using the class lectures to draw this young man to the Savior. He chose to share this saving experience on his final exam booklet. His parents, whom I knew, were ecstatic; praising God for answered prayer and His divine intervention!

That young man continues to serve the Lord. How grateful I am that God would use me, despite my personal "battles," to work in someone else's "kid!" We never know what God is up to! Let us be faithful.

9) *Offer up your children to God, praying that He will restore the years "eaten up" by sinful behavior.*

Although you have upheld Christian precepts and values in your home; remember, that when your child leaves he has already developed his own beliefs and personal agenda. As the prodigal of old who wanted to do his own thing, his father let him go. (cf. Luke 15:11-32)

It's tough when our children fail or make mistakes; but we must commit them to the Lord. Praise God, that the prodigal "came to himself" in repentance and returned home to the father!

10) *Finally, be teachable; God is not through with us yet.*
He will even use our children to develop and train areas of our lives. They are part of us by divine appointment and therefore we need to pay attention. It's an awesome responsibility to raise children in the nurture and admonition of the Lord.
Personally, I thank God for my children and the blessing they have been despite the "difficult" times. They have been used to educate me in my ministry to others. I have come to realize that a Sovereign God has given me the children of His choice and purpose. Through all the trying experiences and joys of parenting, I have come to better understand the father's heart of my Savior. In turn, I have a burden to reach and help the "kids" of this world who

wander about "as sheep without a Shepherd."

REVIEWING THE SUGGESTIONS

* Never give up!

* Intercede for each child daily at the throne of Grace.

* Get rid of all resentment in your heart.

* Maintain a victorious attitude in Christ.

* Enjoy and appreciate your children regardless of their spiritual condition.

* Take the "praise challenge" which is faith in action.

* Be thankful to God for all children who manifest true godliness.

* Be on the lookout for other children who are open for truth.

* Offer up your children to God, praying that He will restore the years "eaten up" by sinful behavior.

* Be teachable, letting God use your children for added personal development.

AN ENCOURAGING CHALLENGE

Beloved parent, it's time to wholly trust the Lord! He is in full control of your life and circumstance. Whatever your home situation, give yourself unreservedly to the Lord Jesus Christ; worship and serve Him whole-heartedly, while trusting the Holy Spirit to seek out your children.

Carry them on your heart in prayer while dropping your burdens at the foot of the Cross. (Philippians 4:4-7)

***Philippians 4:4** Rejoice in the Lord alway: and again I say, Rejoice. **5** Let your moderation be known unto all men. The Lord is at hand. **6** Be careful for nothing; but in every thing by prayer and supplication with thanksgiving let your requests be made known unto God. **7** And the peace of God, which passeth all understanding, shall keep your hearts and minds through Christ Jesus.*

Never give up! And when it appears that nothing is happening, remember the great Spurgeon's words: "When you can't trace God's hand, you can always trust His heart"! Amen!

WHAT GOD HATH PROMISED

God hath not promised skies always blue,
Flower-strewn pathways all our lives through;
God hath not promised sun without rain,
Joy without sorrow, peace without pain.
God hath not promised we shall not know
Toil and temptation, trouble and woe;
He hath not told us we shall not bear
Many a burden, many a care;
God hath not promised smooth roads and wide,
Swift, easy travel, needing no guide;
Never a mountain rocky and steep,
Never a river turbid and deep.
But God hath promised strength for the day,
Rest for the labor, light for the way;

Grace for the trials, help from above,
Unfailing sympathy, undying love!
>   —Annie Johnson Flint

A PARENTAL PRAYER

Thank you, Heavenly Father, that You reign supremely over this universe. Gratefully, we acknowledge Your Sovereignty over our personal world, including our children. We gladly release them to Your divine will and purpose, trusting that one day You will be glorified through each of them.

In the meantime, cause me to be conscious of Your faithful undertaking for my life. Let me revel in Your grace, and may Your joy be my strength.

Please share Your great heart of love with me that I may joyfully walk in truth; thus reflecting the beauty of Your Son. Fill me with the Holy Spirit's wisdom and power that I may properly minister to my family; then use me to make a godly impact for Jesus Christ upon this lost and dying world.

In the Mighty Name of Jesus Christ, Amen.

Joshua's final exhortation to God's people still applies today:

> *"...Choose you this day whom ye will serve... but as for me and my house, we will serve the LORD."* *(Joshua 24:15)*

ABOUT THE AUTHOR

 Pastor, teacher, author, mentor and presently a Bible instructor at the Rescue Mission of Mahoning Valley in Youngstown, Ohio. Bill Finnigan has been engaged in active ministry for over sixty years.

A native of Newark, New Jersey, Bill received a call to ministry while in college. The ensuing years were spent in intensive study to learn and sharpen ministry skills. Attending several universities, he holds a number of degrees, including the Doctor of Ministry. For over twenty-seven years, Bill held pulpits in Pennsylvania and New Jersey, reaching people with God's life-changing Word.

His outreach experience has included radio, prison, and Bible conference ministries. He has served as a college professor, and director of a Biblical counseling center. He has authored other publications, including *Healing for the Mind*, offering comfort and remedy for mental turmoil; *Forgiven to Forgive*, which serves as an antidote to resentment and bitterness; *Living Skillfully,* a commentary on Proverbs; and *Facing Depression*, examining its cause and cure.

More recently his time has been devoted to writing, preaching, and the ongoing instruction at the rescue mission. As the Lord provides opportunities, he continues to be busily engaged in the Lord's Vineyard, considering himself "refired," rather than retired.

Dr. William J. Finnigan
8883 Sherwood Dr. NE
Warren, Ohio 44484
email:bilfinn1@yahoo.com

BOOKS BY Dr. FINNIGAN

1.   A Fresh Look at Pentecost

In Light of Present Day Confusion

If there's been any controversy that has profoundly divided the true Christian Church, it is the question and understanding of what really happened on the Day of Pentecost. This subject is basic to a correct understanding of how the Church began and the subsequent teachings and practices taking us to the present day.

Join Dr. Bill Finnigan as he helps us to look at Pentecost in a fresh and applicable way that will clear up the confusion that is so pervasive in the church today.

2.   Facing Depression

Exploring its Cause and Cure

Depression in America has reached alarming proportions! According to one source, it is estimated that nearly 19 million adults suffer from serious depression, which is almost 10% of the U.S. population. This does not include the millions of teenagers who are depressed and prone to suicide.

In "Facing Depression," Dr. Finnigan presents a thorough examination of the Biblical answer, which is far better than secular solutions.

3.   Living Skillfully
A Practical and Concise Commentary on Proverbs

We live in a confused, lawless world. Many are making a living, but have never learned how to live. This explains, among other things, the rising tide of depression and mental disorders. Knowledge abounds, but how to use that knowledge effectively is another matter; that's where wisdom comes in to play. The Book of Proverbs ("gems of wisdom from God") promotes the skill and common sense to gain God-given success. "Living Skillfully" entails seeing this life from God's perspective, and acting accordingly. What can possibly be more important to equip us for this unique journey on earth?

4.   Forgiven to Forgive

The Cancer of Bitterness

This pamphlet deals with four areas surrounding bitterness and the lack of forgiveness. There is the Cancer of Bitterness, The Cause of Bitterness, The Curse of Bitterness and The Cure for Bitterness. The author addresses the issue from a Biblical basis.

5.   Healing for the Mind

Does the salvation of Jesus Christ include healing for the mind? While the world seems to have gone insane, is there not healing for the mind of the believer? This book is born not from mere academic exercise but from years of spiritual and mental battle. It comes forth to testify that Christ is indeed our "Helmet of Salvation!"

To order Dr. Finnigan's books, go here:

www.billfinnigan.com/books